Christian Crosses

Colouring Book

The Soothing, Simple to Colour
Emblem of the Lord

ESTHER PINCINI

ISBN 978-1-77335-097-4

Magdalene Press, January 2016

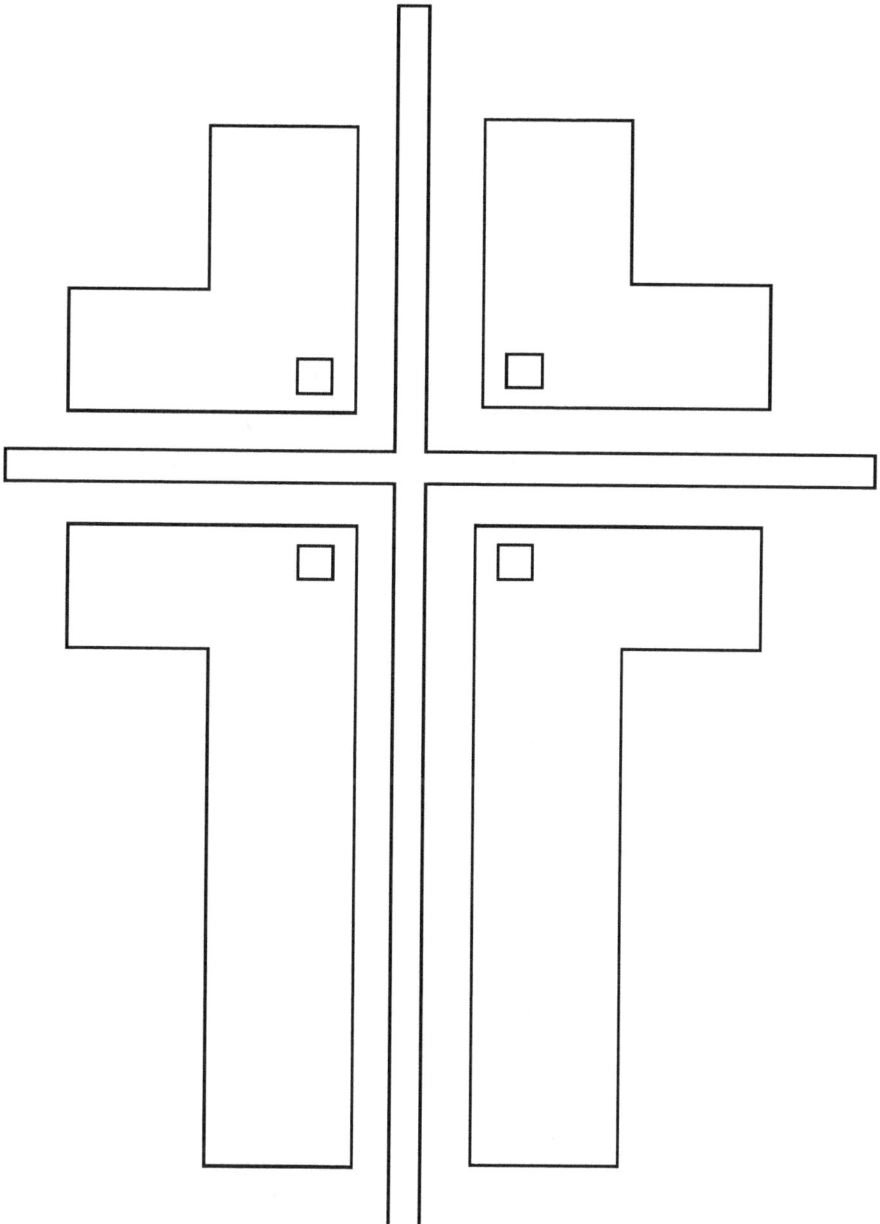

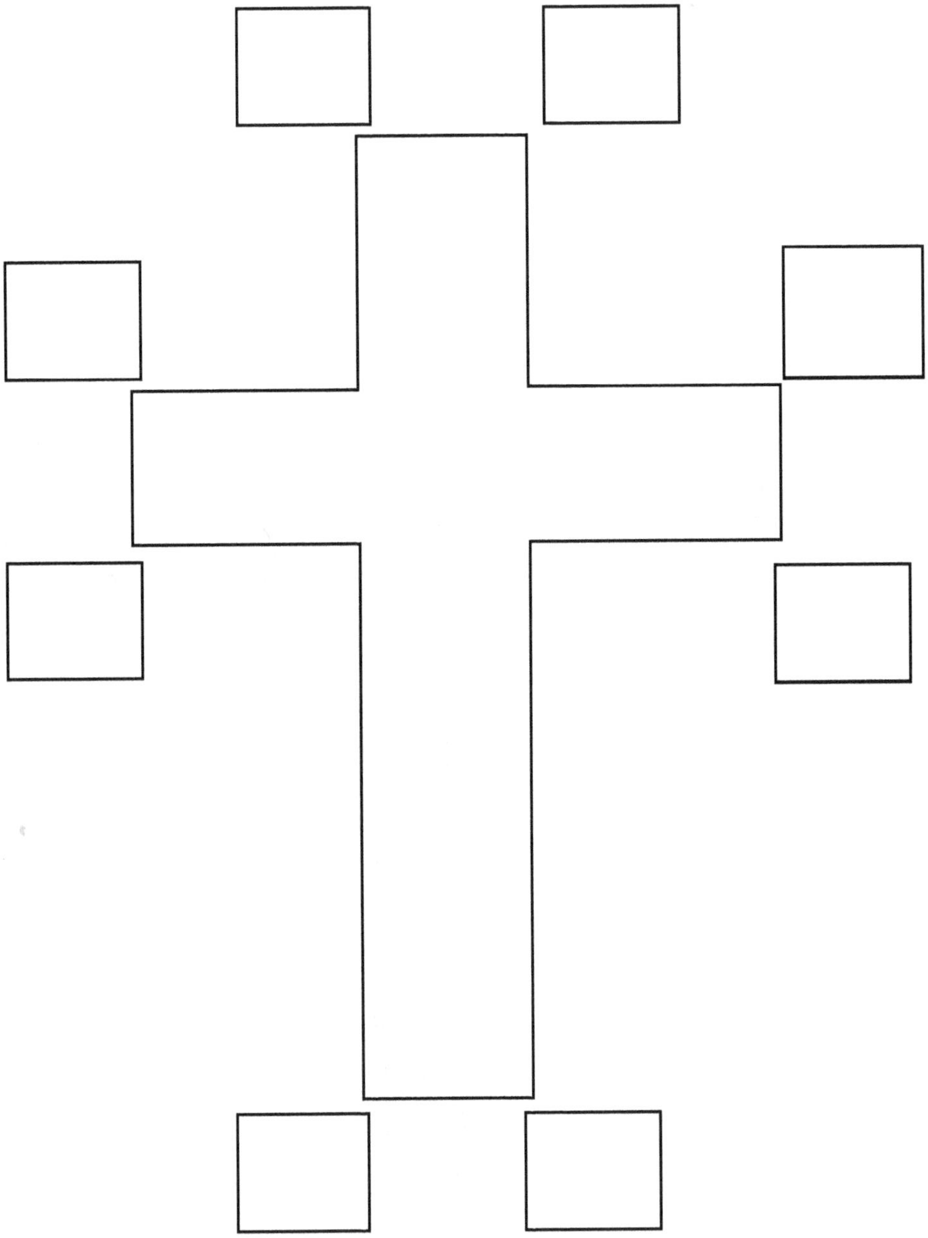

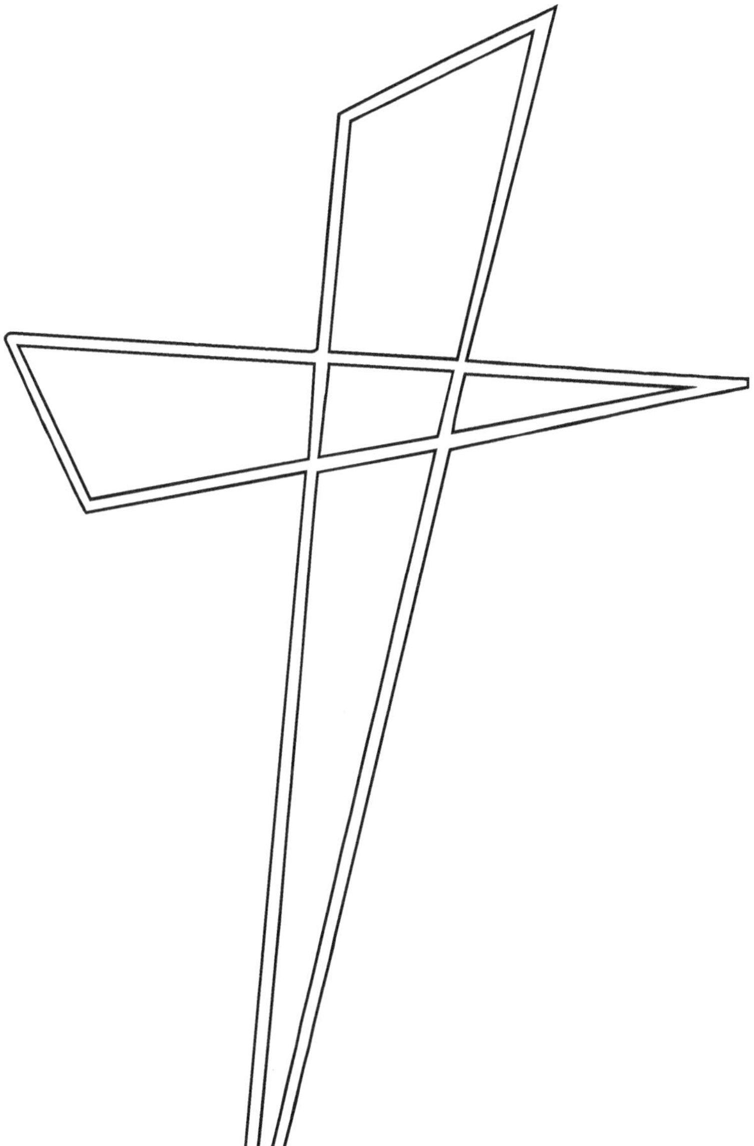

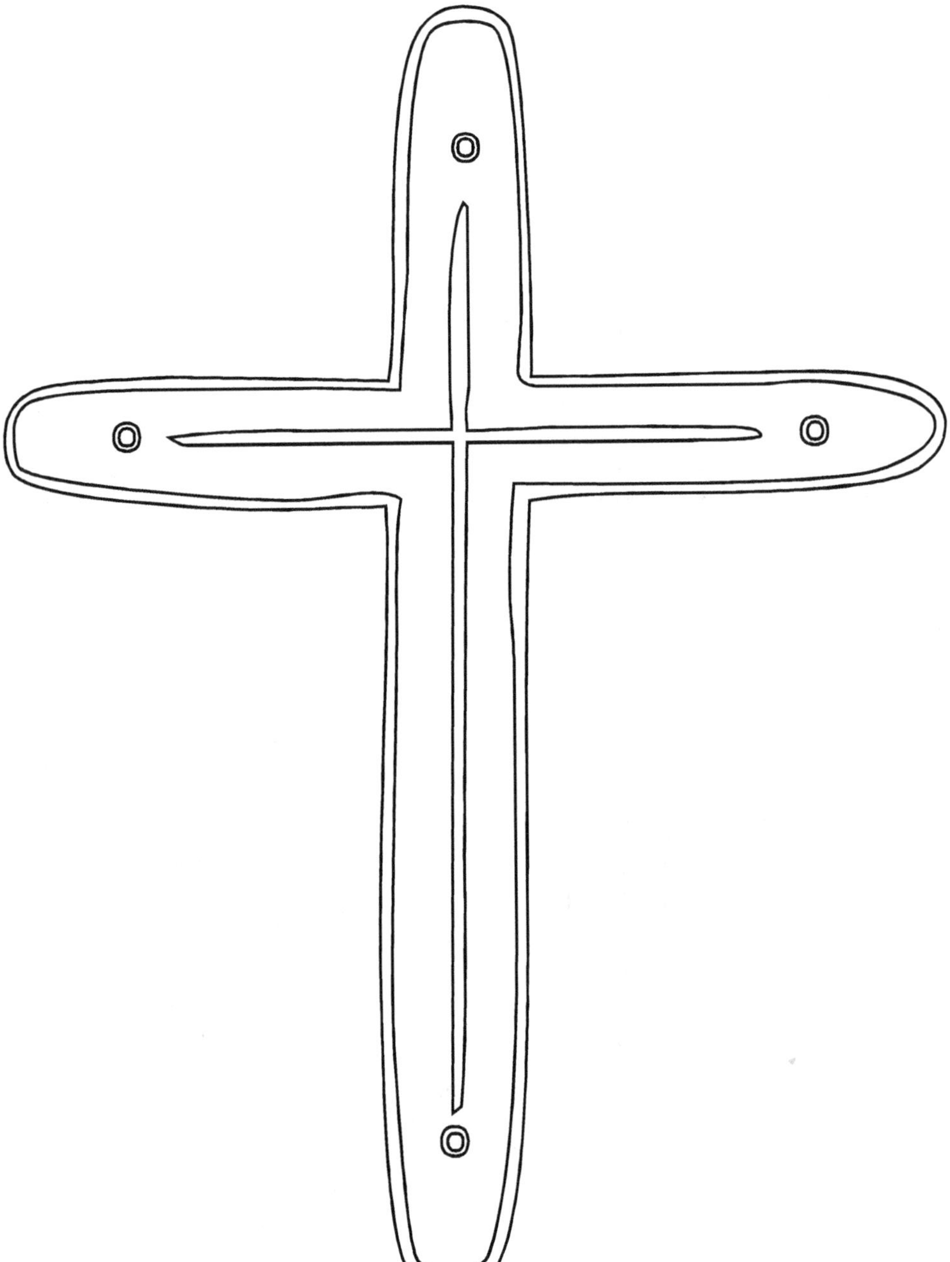

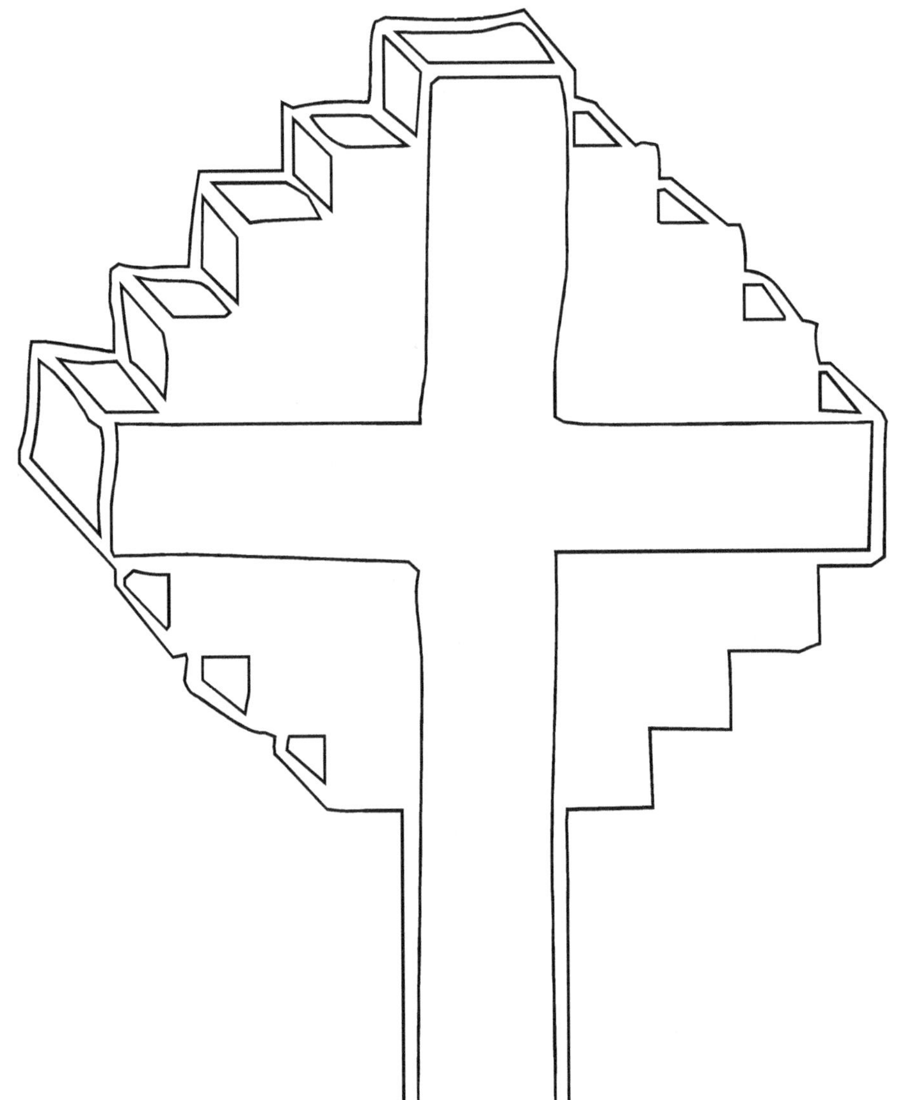

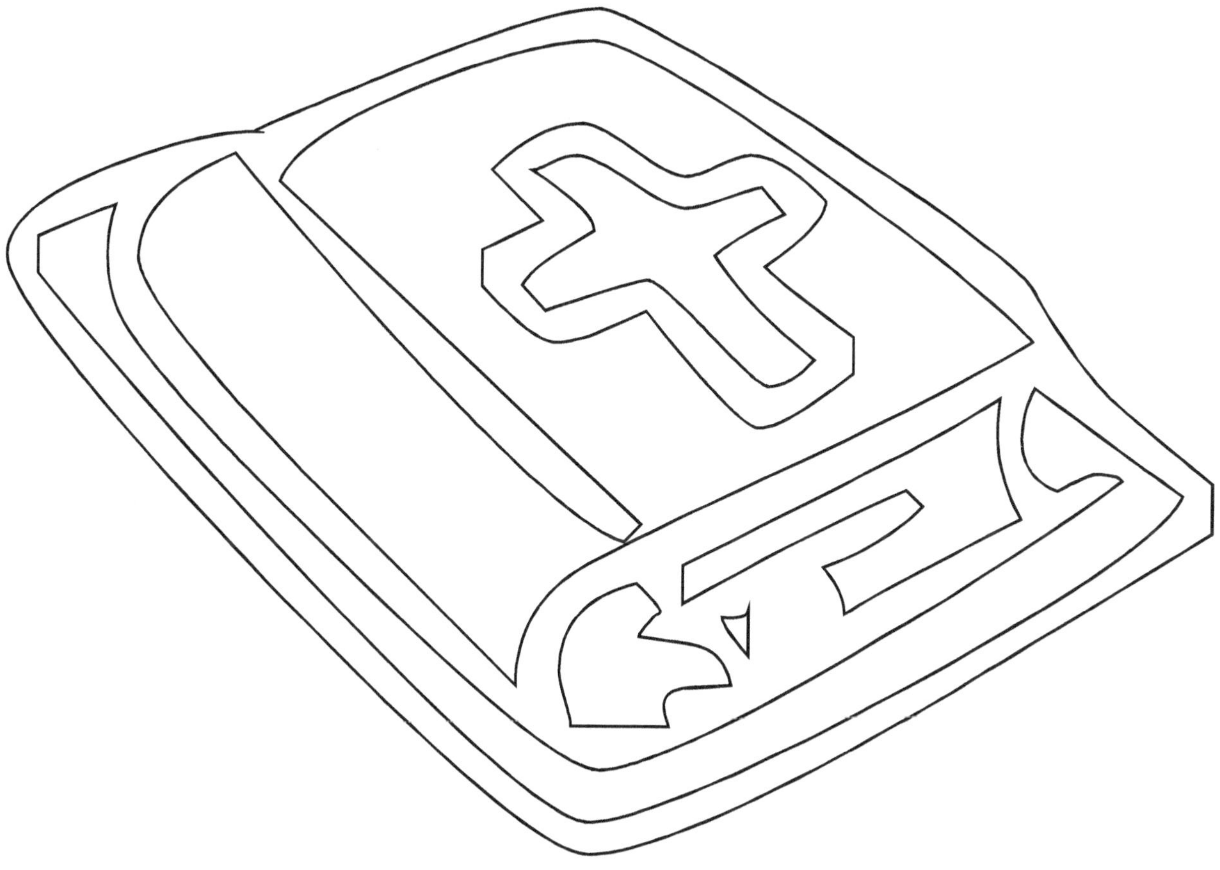

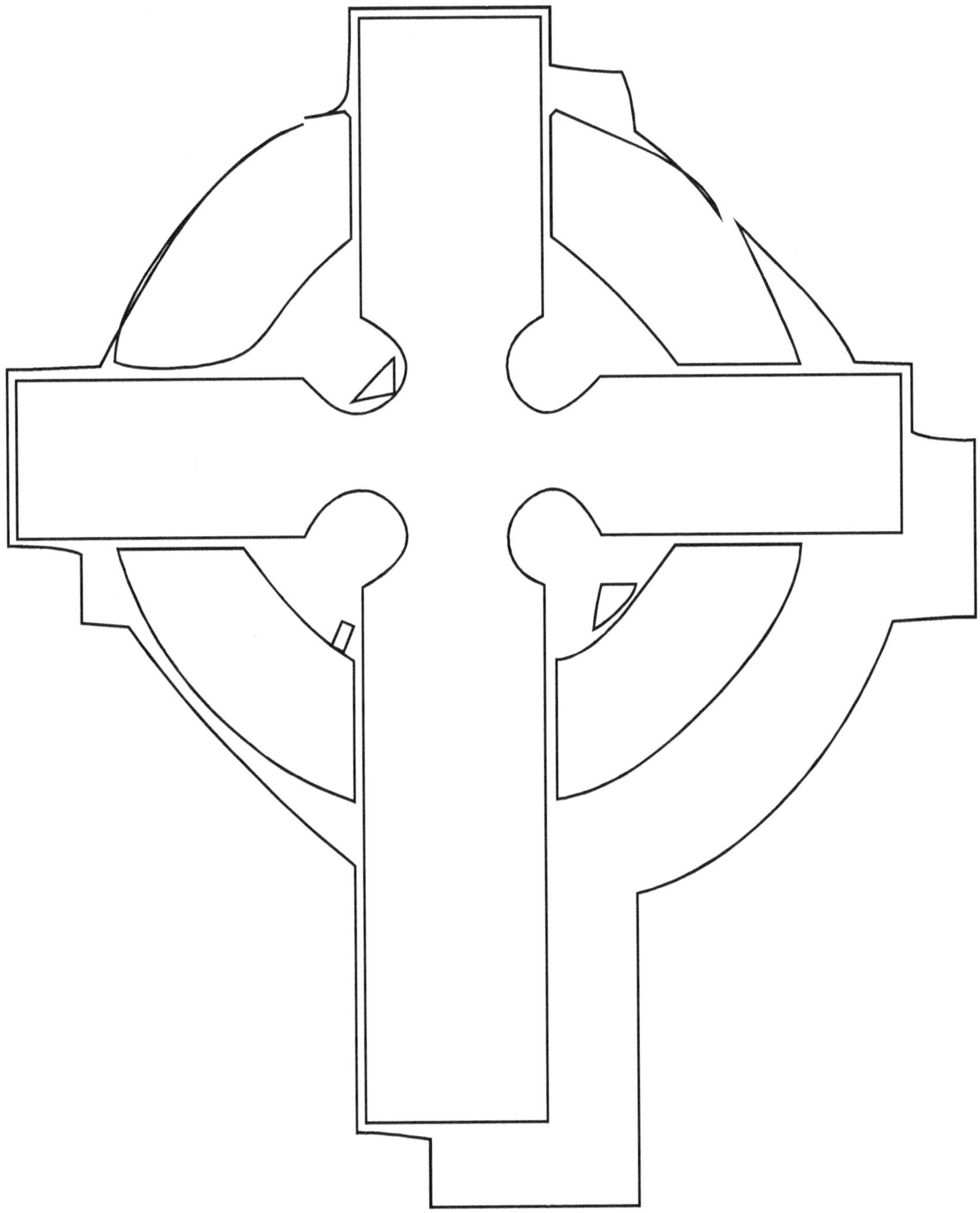

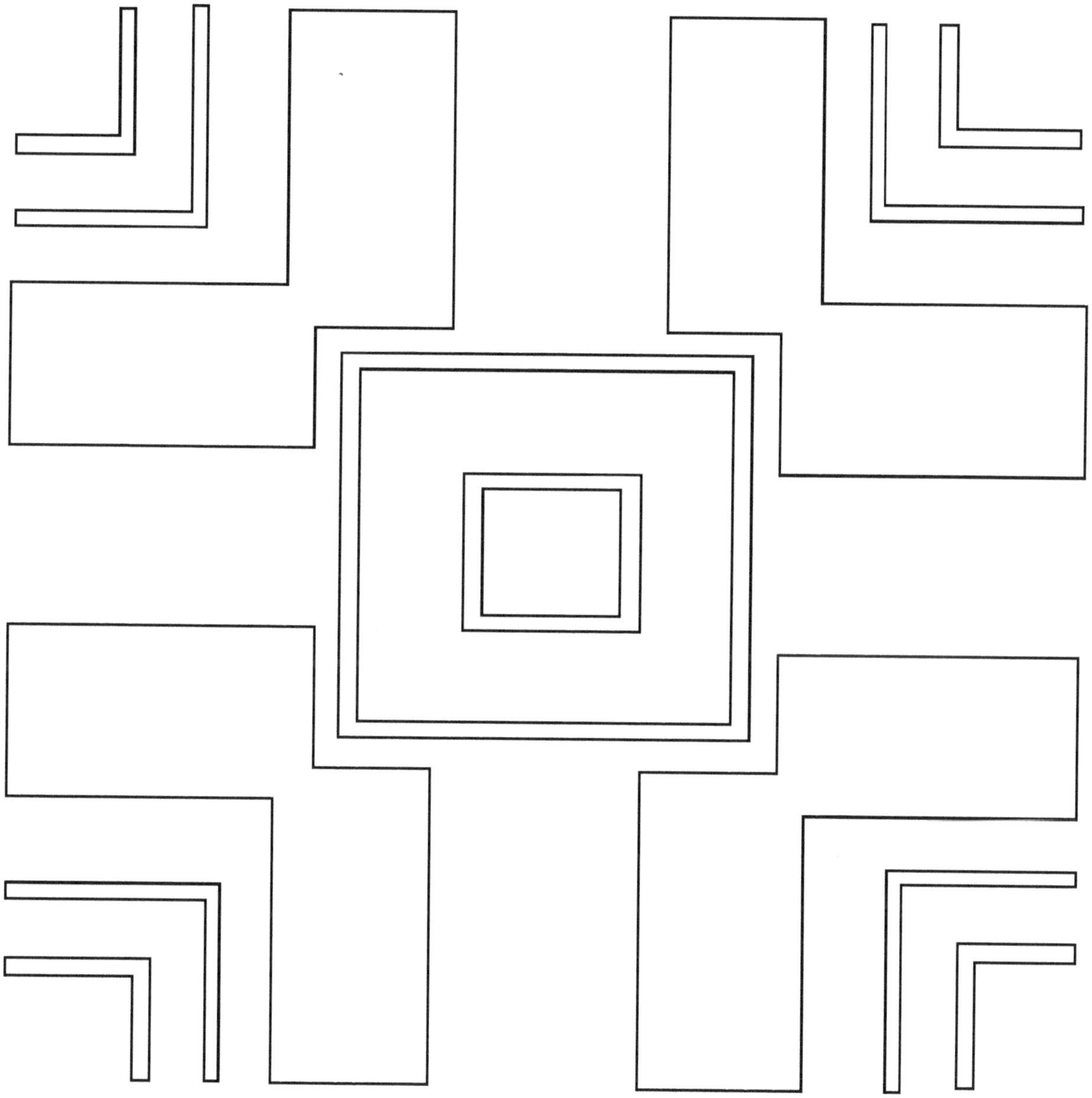

XII

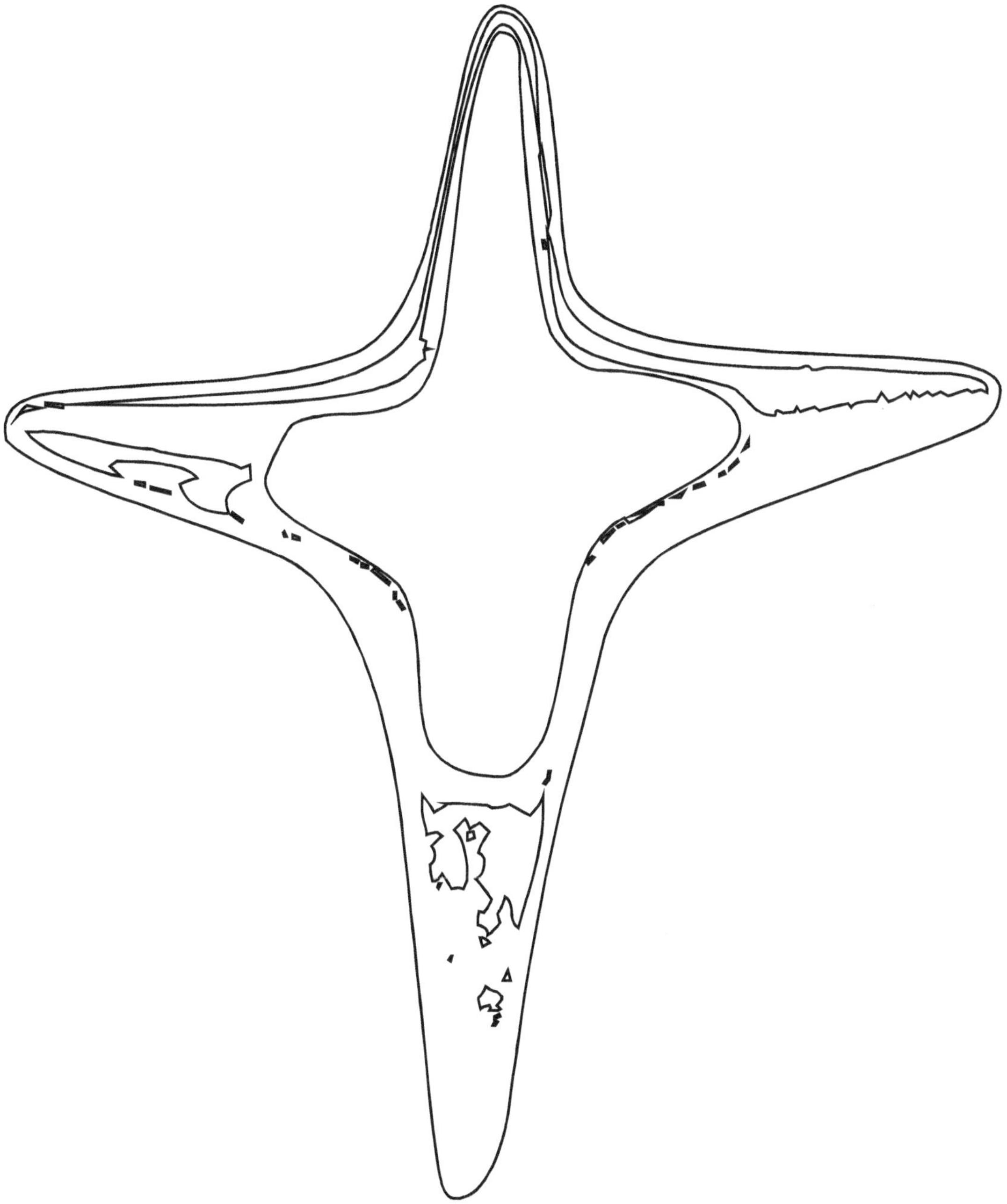

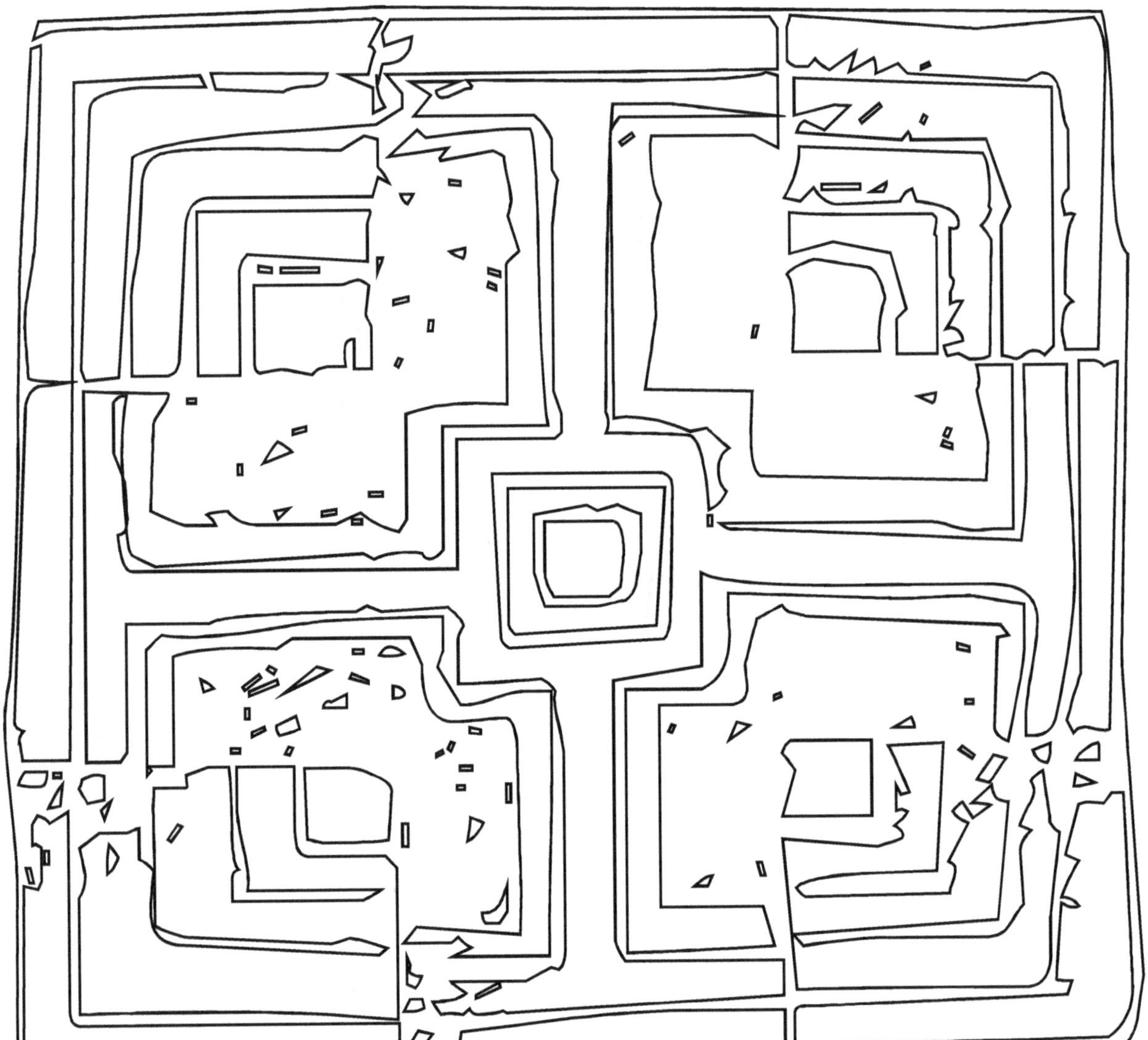

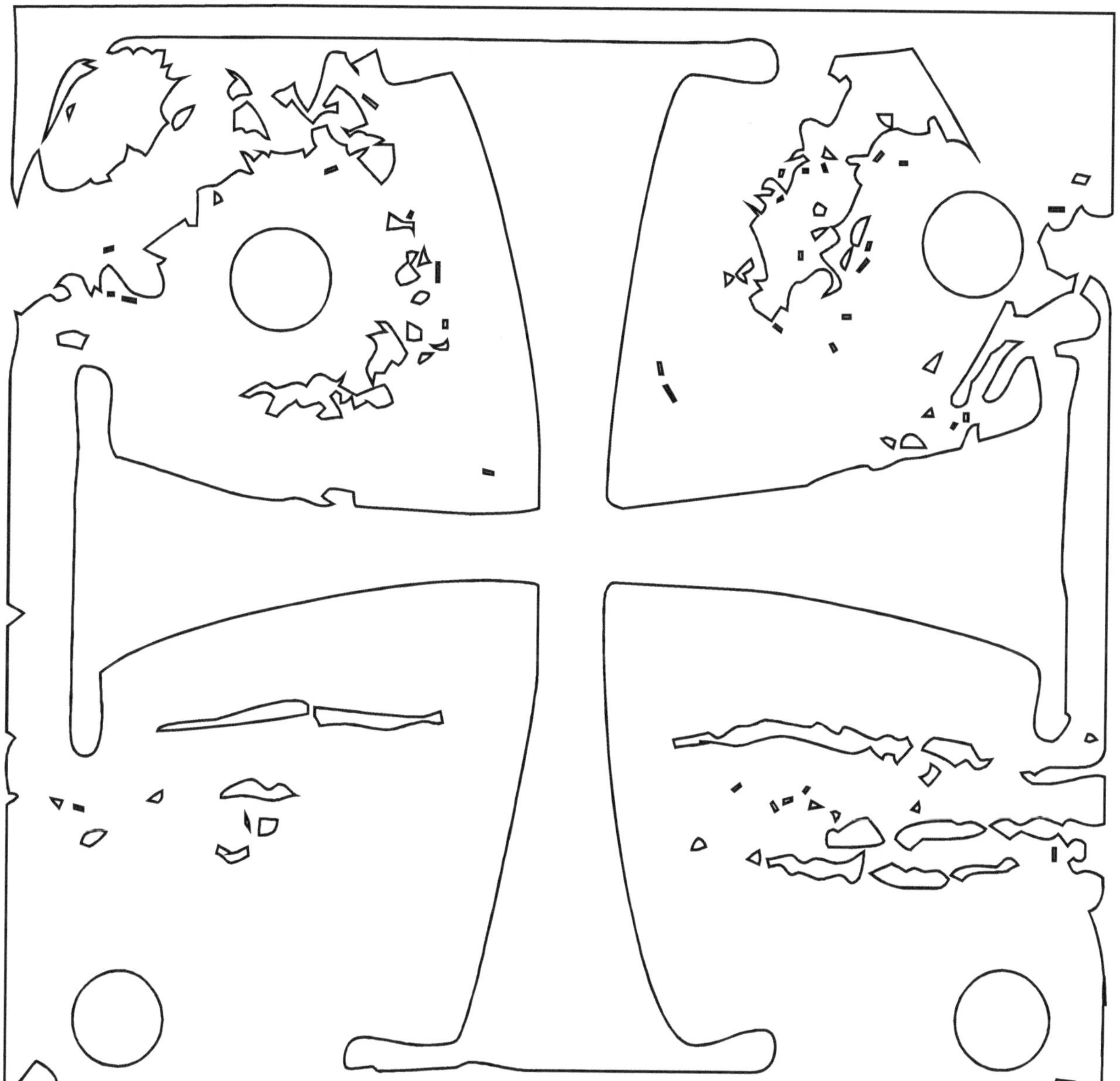

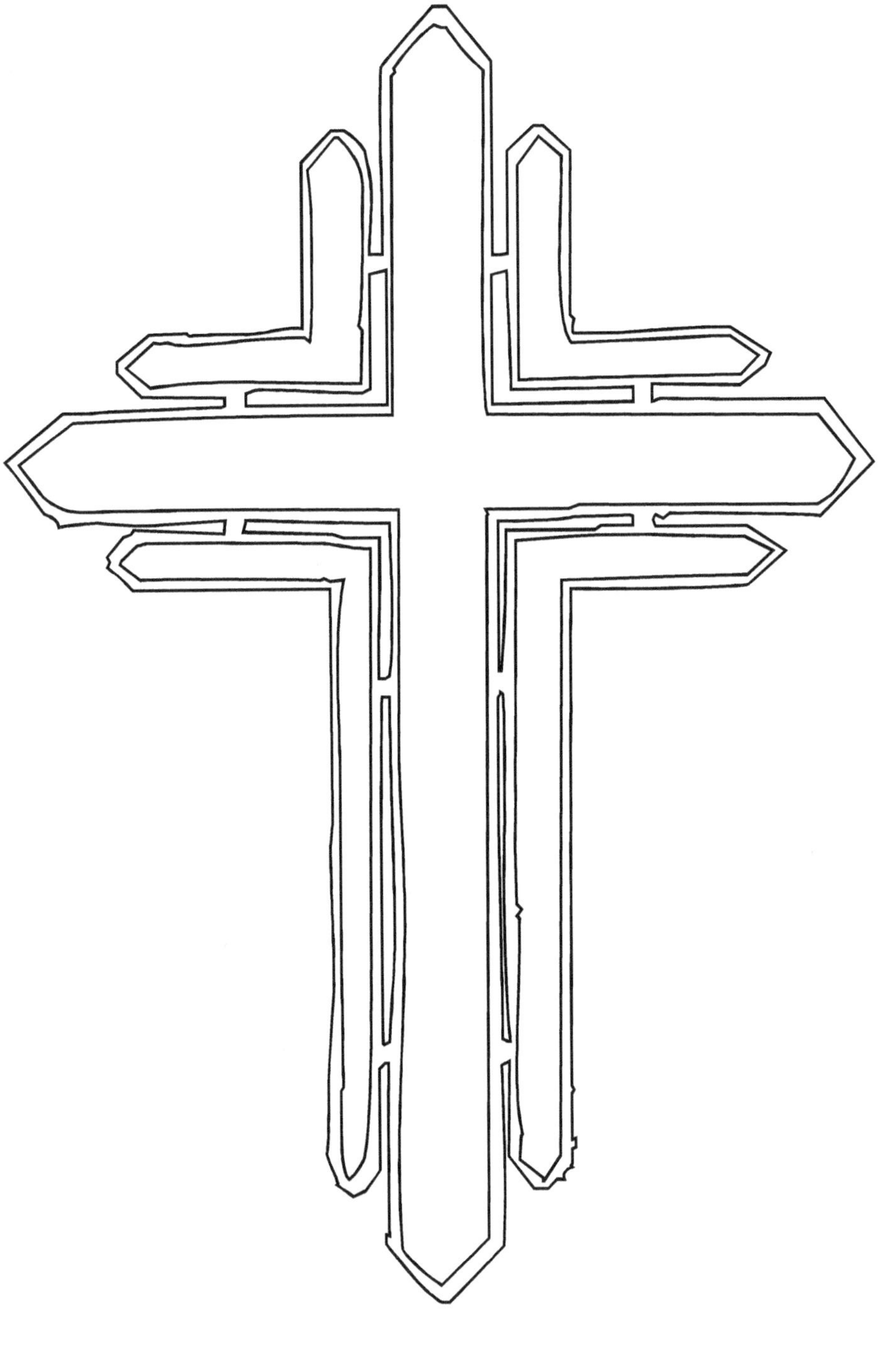

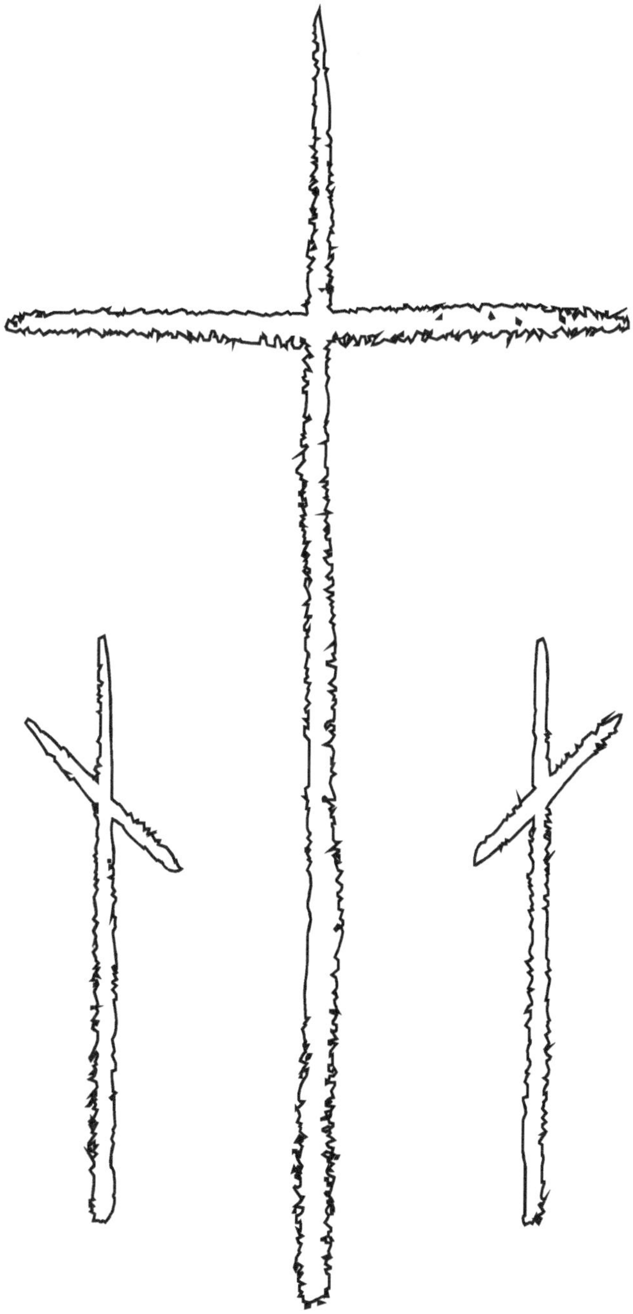

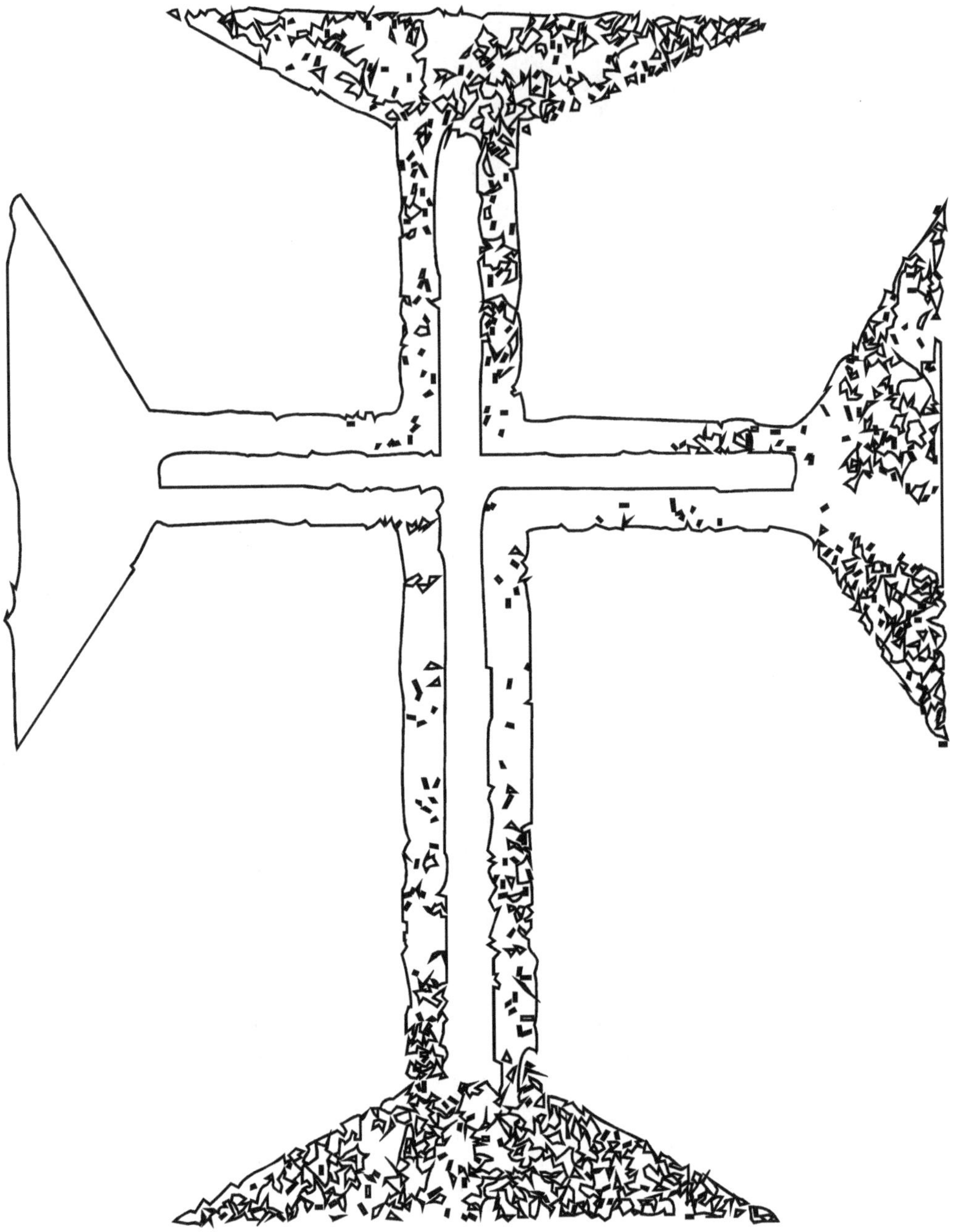

Iesus Nazarenus Rex Iudaeorum

www.ingramcontent.com/pod-product-compliance
Lightning Source LLC
Chambersburg PA
CBHW081228040426
42445CB00016B/1916
* 9 7 8 1 7 7 3 3 5 0 9 7 4 *